♪ ○ Say Can You See ♫

Joe Rhatigan

Reader Consultants

Jennifer M. Lopez, M.S.Ed., NBCT
Senior Coordinator—History/Social Studies
Norfolk Public Schools

Tina Ristau, M.A., SLMS
Teacher Librarian
Waterloo Community School District

iCivics Consultants

Emma Humphries, Ph.D.
Chief Education Officer

Taylor Davis, M.T.
Director of Curriculum and Content

Natacha Scott, MAT
Director of Educator Engagement

Publishing Credits

Rachelle Cracchiolo, M.S.Ed., *Publisher*
Emily R. Smith, M.A.Ed., *VP of Content Development*
Véronique Bos, *Creative Director*
Dona Herweck Rice, *Senior Content Manager*
Dani Neiley, *Associate Content Specialist*
Fabiola Sepulveda, *Series Designer*

Image Credits: p5 Library of Congress (LC-USZ62-53017);
p9, p20 Library of Congress (LC-DIG-ppmsca-3554); p10 Library of Congress
(LC-DIG-ppmsca-23683); p13 right North Wind Picture Archives/Alamy;
p14 Library of Congress (LC-DIG-hec-04307); p15 Library of Congress
(LC-DIG-ds-00032a); p19 Olivier Douliery/ABACAUSA.COM/Newscom;
p21 Library of Congress (LC-DIG-pga-08894); p25 Library of Congress
(LC-100000006) ;all other images from iStock and/or Shutterstock

Library of Congress Cataloging-in-Publication Data

Names: Rhatigan, Joe, author.
Title: O say can you see / Joe Rhatigan.
Description: Huntington Beach : Teacher Created Materials, 2021. | Includes
 index. | Audience: Grades 2-3 | Summary: "Do you know the words to our
 National Anthem? Do you know what those words mean? Find out the story
 behind the song"-- Provided by publisher.
Identifiers: LCCN 2020043721 (print) | LCCN 2020043722 (ebook) | ISBN
 9781087605005 (paperback) | ISBN 9781087620022 (ebook)
Subjects: LCSH: Star-spangled banner (Song)--Juvenile literature. |
 Baltimore, Battle of, Baltimore, Md., 1814--Juvenile literature. | Key,
 Francis Scott, 1779-1843--Juvenile literature.
Classification: LCC ML3561.S8 R53 2021 (print) | LCC ML3561.S8 (ebook) |
 DDC 782.421/5990973--dc23
LC record available at https://lccn.loc.gov/2020043721
LC ebook record available at https://lccn.loc.gov/2020043722

5482 Argosy Avenue
Huntington Beach, CA 92649-1039
www.tcmpub.com

ISBN 978-1-0876-0500-5

Table of Contents

What's the Story?

You might know that the national **anthem** of the United States is "The Star-**Spangled** Banner." You may have sung it. Do you know all the words? Do you know what they mean?

What about the song's history? You might know that it was written by Francis Scott Key. But have you heard the rest of the story behind the words?

It began with a war. A war that the United States was losing.

Francis Scott Key

Jump into Fiction

Gallantly Streaming?

It's a bright, sunny day at the baseball field. Dennis takes off his cap for the national anthem. He holds the hat over his heart and tries to sing along.

"O say can you see! By the dawn's early light! What so proudly we... um, er, uh... gleaming," Dennis sings.

"*Gallantly streaming?* What in the world is going on in this song anyway?" he wonders.

The last words, "home of the brave," ring out. "The song has bombs, rockets, and a flag," Dennis says to his friend Andy. "It has to be a song about a war."

But now, it's time to play ball!

After the game, Dennis goes home and looks up the national anthem. Soon, he finds a video about the event the song describes.

Dennis imagines he's there as he watches the video. He sees a fort and lots of ships in the harbor. He sees a man pacing back and forth on a ship deck. British sailors are rushing around him. They are getting ready for a battle. And after the battle, the flag still waves.

Dennis feels excited and proud as he learns. Gallantly streaming? The flag sure was!

Dennis can't wait to tell Andy all about it. And he'll be sure to know all the words at the next ball game!

Back to Nonfiction

The Battle of Baltimore

The year was 1814. Francis Scott Key was on a mission to help his friend. The United States was at war against Britain. It wasn't going well. The British had attacked Washington, DC. And now, they were trying to destroy Fort McHenry. The fort protected the city of Baltimore. If they got in, the British would be one step closer to winning.

the White House in the early 1800s

Key, an American, was caught on a British ship. His friend had been **captured**. Key was trying to get the British to let his friend go. They had finally reached an agreement. But then Key was told they couldn't leave the ship. The British were about to attack! They were stuck.

Fort McHenry

Fort McHenry is shaped like a **pentagon**. It is still standing. It is a national monument and historic site.

It was a scary time in the country. People were worried that the fort wouldn't make it through the night. They were worried the country would no longer be free.

The ship Key was on was not close to the fort. In fact, Key couldn't really see the fort.

The sky grew dark. The ships fired their bombs and rockets. The battle lasted all night. At times, the explosions were bright. Key could see the fort's flag. If the U.S. flag stayed flying, he knew the Americans hadn't given up. But if he saw a white flag, that would mean they had **surrendered**.

This is what Fort McHenry looks like today.

By the Numbers

The British had about 19 ships.
There were 1,000 American soldiers
in the fort. The British launched
about 2,000 bombs and rockets.

The attack stopped in the early morning. Key waited for the mist and the smoke to clear. When it did, he saw the American flag! The fort had survived the battle. The British had lost. They gave up the fight for the fort.

The next day, Key wrote a poem on the back of a letter he had in his pocket. The poem was about how he felt when he saw that flag still flying. The experience filled him with pride and **patriotism**. And the words of the poem reflect that today.

the original copy of Key's poem, which became the words of the national anthem

Think and Talk

Can you tell from this picture what Key feels as he sees the flag still flying?

Understanding the Words

> *O say can you see, by the dawn's early light,*
>
> *What so proudly we hail'd at the twilight's last gleaming*

These are the first two lines of the poem. What do they mean? Key wrote about the morning after the battle. *By the dawn's early light* means as the sun rises.

But Key is asking, "*O say can you see...what so proudly we hail'd...?*" Key is talking to the listener. He asks if they can see the flag that was proudly honored, or *hail'd*. He asks because the flag was there the day before at the *twilight's last gleaming*. This means as the sun set. In other words, can you see the flag this morning that we honored yesterday?

> *Whose broad stripes and bright stars through the perilous fight,*
>
> *O'er the ramparts we watch'd were so gallantly streaming?*

In these lines, Key is describing the flag's stripes and stars. *So gallantly streaming* means the flag flew bravely. He says that the flag flew throughout the dangerous battle, or *the **perilous fight***. And he describes where the flag could be seen. *O'er the **ramparts*** means it was high above the fort walls.

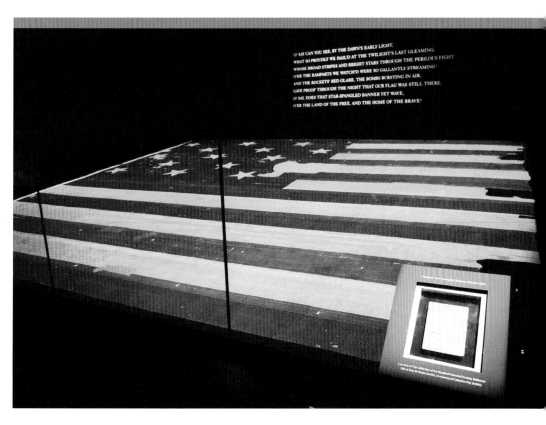

Still Waving

The flag today has 13 stripes and 50 stars. In 1814, the fort's flag had 15 stars and 15 stripes. This flag still exists. You can see it at a museum in Washington, DC.

And the rocket's red glare, the bombs bursting in air,

Gave proof through the night that our flag was still there

These lines might be easier to understand. The flag was a **symbol** of hope. How could Key see it during the night? He could see it by the light of explosions, or the *rocket's red glare.* This was how he could tell that the fort had not surrendered.

drawing of the bombs at Fort McHenry

There's More?

The original title of Key's poem is "Defence of Fort M'Henry." There are four verses. But the song sung most of the time is only the first verse.

> *O say does that star-spangled banner yet wave*
> *O'er the land of the free and the home of the brave?*

The final two lines ask a question. But they could be asking more than one question. Does the flag still fly over the United States? Is it still *the land of the free and the home of the brave*? Are the people still proud of their country?

It is important to note that at the time Key wrote, not all people were free. Many were enslaved people. Did he mean all people in "the land of the free"? No matter what he meant, all people are included now.

Think and Talk

What does this picture show us about how people may feel about the flag and song?

Home of the Brave

Today, people sing the anthem in school. It is sung at sporting events. Some people sing it on the Fourth of July. And now, you know its story.

The song is more than just something people sing. It is a symbol of hope. It was for brave people like the soldiers who fought against the British. It is for the soldiers who fight today.

The song is for people who love the country and what it stands for. It is for the people who dream of what the country can be. Most of all, it is for all the people of the United States of America.

Official Anthem

"The Star-Spangled Banner" was well known for a long time. But it was not always the national anthem. That did not happen until 1931.

Glossary

anthem—a patriotic song

captured—taken or kidnapped

patriotism—love for one's country

pentagon—a shape that has five sides and
  five angles

perilous—dangerous

ramparts—protective walls

spangled—decorated

surrendered—given up

symbol—something that stands for
  something else

Index

Civics in Action

The words to "The Star-Spangled Banner" can be tricky to learn. But they are also important to know. People join together to sing the words. Knowing and singing the anthem may help a person feel patriotic. You can learn the words too!

1. Write the words to the anthem. Just writing the words will help you to learn them.

2. Find a recording of the anthem. This is easy to find online. A grown-up can help you.

3. Every day, listen to the anthem and read and sing along.

4. After a few days, you will probably have learned the anthem by heart. Now, sing it without reading it!